D0594553

Presented To

Regina

Stay, blessed and forever encouraged as you are Grieving Under Grace!

From

Deborah Irye

Date

March 21, 2019

Grieving Under Grace
"God's Reachable Anointing Covers Everyone."

Copyright © 2018 Deborah Juniper-Frye
All Rights Reserved.

Published by:
Amazon Publishing Company

All rights reserved. No part of this book may be used, reproduced, uploaded, stored or introduced into a retrieval system, or transmitted in any way or by any means, including electronic, mechanical, recording, or otherwise, without the permission of the publisher, except by the reviewer who may quote brief passages in a review. Copying of this book is illegal and unethical.

ISBN-13:978-1981462797
ISBN-10:1981462791

Copyright © 2018 Deborah Juniper-Frye
All Rights Reserved.

Printed in the United States of America

Foreword

For the last three decades, one of my primary roles has been walking with people through their grief and helping them find closure. Often, a measure of that closure has come at the homegoing or funeral services we conduct here at our church. For nearly twenty years, Deborah Juniper-Frye has assisted me in helping families recover from the deep loss of their loved ones. Her book, *Grieving Under Grace*, carries with it years of actual experience with real families handling real losses. Let it minister to your need today, and please never forget that He comforts those who are broken by grief with His grace.

B. Courtney McBath, D. Min
Calvary Revival Church
Norfolk, Virginia

Acknowledgments

With a jubilant shout, I can say that procrastination, doubt, and fear did not hold me back from accomplishing the dream I had tucked away in me for some years; publishing my first book. It has been an overcoming journey that has set me on a path to continue breaking the barriers stacked before me and continue to change the dynamics of my family.

First and foremost, I would like to dedicate my first of many books to my parents, Francis and Corrine Juniper. To this day, I live as if they are watching and cheering me on from their vantage point. I can see my father, watching me from the baseball fence, as he did when I was a little girl playing softball, and I can hear my mother saying, "Go ahead, Deborah!" I also dedicate and pledge this book, *Grieving Under Grace* to my siblings who are no longer here; until we meet again.

Secondly, can I just say, "I Love Michael Frye!!!" He has been my rock, my confidant, my biggest supporter, and my #1 Fan. Even when I had moments of doubt, his love has been a great source of encouragement. He was such a wonderful provoker of insight and motivation, and helped me to cultivate my thoughts and ideas throughout this process. Michael has been instrumental from the beginning to the end, and I dedicate this book to him, My Love.

To my children, my siblings, and my entire family ~ I thank you. To all of my encouragers, my girlfriends, and supporters ~ I thank you. To my pastors and church family ~ I thank you. To all of the seniors who have shared their wisdom and grace ~ I thank you. To the numerous families who have given me the opportunity to assist them through this grief journey ~ I thank you. To my Life Transformational Coach, Latrece Williams-McKnight ~ I thank you. To the One who has made all of this possible, God Almighty ~ I THANK YOU!

The Introduction

When I was a little girl, we lived down the street from a funeral home. My friends and I would go to the funeral home to look around and see if there were any dead people in there. We would cling to one another scared to death ourselves but determined to be braver than each other. In my younger years, when attending a funeral, I would be the one who the church female usher would have to give tissue to, and someone would have to get me back to the vehicle because I was so upset. As I look back over the years, there is no doubt that God has helped me to overcome that fear and has given me the gift of compassion and care for the grieving and brokenhearted.

Finally, as Oprah would say, "I had the Aha Moment!" I had been pondering a name to call my grief business for a few years, but rarely told anyone. I would speak with my husband and close friends about stepping out but was too afraid to try. During the Saturday of the Glow 2017 Conference, after listening to all of the wonderful and inspirational speakers, I whispered in my Pastor Janeen's ear that she was looking at a business owner and author ~ we both broke down and cried. I had to do something, so I began seriously talking to my Coach, Latrece Williams-McKnight about the burning desire to really do this, and of course, it was on and popping from that point on.

I went home that night of September 16, 2017, and sat in the middle of the bed with a pen and paper, and said, "God, ok give me the title you want me to write about?" I stayed still, meditating, one eye open, one eye closed; one hour went by, and then another hour went by. I said, "Lord Mercy, it's almost midnight, but I'm not going to bed Lord until you speak." I started praying, Holy Spirit, give me ears to hear and a heart to receive what God will say. It was just after midnight on Sunday, September 17th, that God whispered the title, "Grieving Under Grace." I immediately shared the title with Michael, started praising and thanking God, and went out like a light.

Listen, the next morning, as Michael and I were riding to church, I thought out loud, *What would be the names of my chapter titles?* I heard the still voice again, "Your chapters titles will be about various grief, all of which you have faced and are going through right now, start writing." I scrambled for a piece of paper (an old bill) and something to write with, and I quickly wrote down 8-chapter titles and came to a stop. I said, "Ok God, I need two more." That still voice again said, "No, 8 is all you need." I looked up the meaning of the number 8, to see that it's the number of NEW BEGINNINGS.

At this point, I was overwhelmed with tears, ran into the church, and made a beeline to find Latrece to show her what God has given me within our 15-minute ride to church. For weeks, I was stuck on the #8 and asked God, "Please give me more insight, why just 8?" As I was brushing my teeth and looking in the mirror, He said,

"You will launch your business and book in 2018.
You are the 8th child born to your parents.
You were born in the 8th month on the 18th day.
The number 8 is significant in your life."

Needless to say, I was outdone; toothpaste was everywhere. LOL!!!

I believe we can all agree that grief is something we have experienced in one way or another. It is my earnest prayer that you can identify with and gain a positive perspective of "Grieving Under Grace." I tell people all the time, grief is something we have learned to manage on a daily basis, but don't realize it because we have been so conditioned to only see the loss of a loved one as grief. Let's take this journey together and put everything that we are grieving over, under Grace. Continue to stay blessed and forever encouraged.

Table of Contents

Chapter One

Grieving Over Terminal Illness

"Loving Them to Life."

Terminal Illness ~ an incurable disease that cannot be adequately treated and is reasonably expected to result in the death of the patient within a short period of time. Wikipedia Definition

Terminal illness is different from other diseases; you have to get in touch with your own feelings before you can start helping your loved one or anyone else. You will go through so many different emotions such as, "anger," "denial," and "helplessness," to name a few. You feel as if you have absolutely no control. You go from saying, "This is not happening," to saying, "This is happening, how can I stop this?" Hearing the words, "You have a terminal illness," can be the most shocking and unimaginable news ever, you have 3 months, 6 months, or 9 months to live. Most people will go home to handle end of life business, which I call, 'death business.' However, let's think for a minute, how many of us ponder, instead of death business, let's prepare for more life business, making more lasting memories, and sharing life to the fullest ~ until death do us part.

There are stages you will find yourself in, such as praying for healing, praying for keeping power, praying through the fight to keep your loved one here, to finally, loving them so much, that you "Love Them To Life!" We have to ask God for the will to allow His will to be done; God knows it's not easy. You may find yourself in the state of mind to pray, "God just take them, don't allow them to suffer another day." It's not giving up; it's giving into Peace, Assurance, and Unselfishness.

Loving and caring for someone with a terminal illness is just an overwhelming task and seems to be an unfair journey. From the young to the old, it's very difficult to endure unless you know where to pull that inner strength and courage from. We must know where that GRACE comes from; it is dispatched straight from Heaven. As I mentioned, terminal illness care is daunting, to say the least, but watching a mother, father, or grandparents caring for a child with a terminal illness is gut-wrenching, yet soul-stirring. On several occasions, God has allowed me to witness the supernatural calmness and grace that hovers a home where a terminally ill child is serenaded into the arms of Jesus, or prayers going up to heaven that silence the hospital machines in the room, or seeing a father put clean pajamas on his daughter, before she is removed from the home. Lord Mercy.

Just before my mother, Sweet Corrine, became very ill, my sisters and I went to check out some nursing facilities to move her to, but my Mama was not having it! In her not so Sweet Corrine voice, she said, "There are 10 of y'all, and you gonna take care of me at home!" Like she said, it was 10 of us, and my Mama did not have a whole lot of time for sweet talk, she gave a direction, and you had better move, or see a shoe, a belt buckle, or a 5 twist switch coming your way. Therefore, when the time came, there were no questions asked, Mama would be spending her last days at home.

Communication and staying in reality is the key; death was coming, and you have to talk about it. The best thing we can do for our family or children, is to talk about our last party, here on earth! It's called a Pre-Need Arrangement, going to your favorite Funeral Home and setting the stage for your final party. My plan is to go out with a BANG for little to no money out of my family's pocket. My family already knows we are not paying thousands of dollars for dirt and burying nothing. We tend to think, if we speak about it, we are cursing ourselves or speeding up our deaths. God has control of all of that, let Him handle it.

We came together as a family and supported our mother's wishes as best we could. Our mother's death transformed our family dynamics. We learned to care for one another, as we cared for Mama. We had meals together, we laughed with each other, encouraged one another, and we grew to tolerate and show more respect for one another. A lengthy illness can give a family time to see the best in each other, as well as be a platform for forgiveness and renewed love for one another.

It's very important not to let dying get in the way of living. You have to be very careful not to let this part of the journey paralyze you, keep you in a deep depression, or become bewildered in the process. The better you care for yourself, the better you will care for your sweet loved one. Don't get me wrong, planning for a glorious homegoing is very important, but it should not take up the last good days you have here on this side of heaven, with those you genuinely love. "How about we come up with something that's called a "Bucket List?" Bucket List ~ a number of experiences or achievements that a person hopes to have accomplished during their lifetime. Here is another definition ~ a list of things that one has not done but wants to do before dying (Merriam-Webster Dictionary). Your Bucket List is unique to you and can be customized to your liking. If you don't have a list, you can Google some ideas. I told my husband that for one of my bucket list items, I would like to learn how to speak fluent Spanish. Of course, he had jokes and said, "Honey, you are just learning how to speak good English." LOL!

As you can see, at this ending stage of life, the last months of your life can be the best months of someone else' life. It's the small things that comforts the most ~ soft sweet music in the room to set a glorious atmosphere, sweet whispers, hugs, kisses, smiles, seeing family together, and whatever else you can think of to bring peace and joy for a glorious transition from this earth to Heaven, directly into the loving Arms of Jesus. So, at the end of this life

11

journey, let's make it our mission to ***Love Them to Life***.

> # Grace Nugget
>
> ~
>
> *"Death has a way of making you do things, you had no thought of doing in the beginning."*

Grace Moment

Lord,
Please help me to bring comfort where there is pain, courage where there is fear, hope where there is despair, acceptance when the end is near, and a gentle touch of tenderness, patience, and love.

-Amen

Grace Reflections (Notes)

Grace Reflections (Cont'd)

Grace Reflections (Cont'd)

_____

_____

_____

_____

_____

_____

_____

_____

_____

_____

_____

_____

_____

_____

_____

_____

Grace Reflections (Cont'd)

_____

_____

_____

_____

_____

_____

_____

_____

_____

_____

_____

_____

_____

_____

_____

_____

Chapter Two

Grieving Over the Unexpected

"When Option One Is Gone."

Unexpected Grief ~ unforeseen, unanticipated, unpredicted, sudden, abrupt, surprising, unannounced, an unexpected thing. (Merriam-Webster Dictionary)

When I think of this subject, my thoughts are almost endless. We can all make up a list that would stretch a mile down the street, with our own personal "unexpected grief." My thoughts took me straight to things like ~ sexual abuse, drug addiction, prison incarceration, family mistakes, divorce, and world tragedies, just to name a few. We all can compile our own lifelong list. What's on your list? In pondering over any one of these unexpected griefs too long, we can surely, most definitely find ourselves in a self-made hole, covering ourselves up, until we think these things have gone away!

What do we do, When Option One Is Gone? You can't pray the situation away, you can't wish the situation away, you can't cover it up, you can't act like you don't see it, feel it, or know about it. It's looking you square in the face. Again, what do you do when you can't change a thing about this "unexpected grief?" If we think about it, just about every day, there can be something that happens that we just don't expect, and it doesn't have to be up in our face or earth-shattering. It can be something minor that can cause unexpected grief and turmoil. In doing some research (https://www.linkedin.com), I've learned that unexpected grief can be dealt with in a few ways, depending on several things ~ your attitude, acceptance, finding the best balance to deal with the issue, or being determined to use it as a learning tool of progress.

The bottom line is, we will all face these challenges and the quickest thing to do is to Get Yourself Together! It's like the instruction we receive when we are flying ~ not to pass out and to help others, you must put your oxygen mask on first. Catch your breath, dig into your inner strength, face the adversity, be resilient, and for your sake, focus on the renewed peace and joy that you will need for this journey. When I think about all of these ups and downs, I think of the toy so many of us have played with ~ a Kaleidoscope, a constantly changing pattern or sequence of objects or elements. We must become that continuous change of balance.

Now listen, all of this is so much easier said than done, it's daily, and most of the time, a very uncomfortable process. I have found that the process of grieving can be very isolating (to set apart from others, quarantine ~ Merriam Webster Dictionary). We walk around all dressed up with a kool-aid smile on our face, but on the inside, we are the loneliest person in the world. Most of the time, isolation is self-imposed due to our own feelings of anger, sadness, mistrust, helplessness, anxiety, or depression. All of these emotions are normal and at times warranted, but we cannot allow these possible long-term emotions to be our unhealthy guide or keep us hostage.

The phenomenal thing about unexpected grief is that no one has to do this alone, NO ONE. I genuinely believe that through this difficult journey, we must find our HOT SPOT ~ "However, Over Time (HOT)" Spot. However, Over Time, this too shall pass; However, Over Time, I will find renewed joy; However, Over Time, God will see me through. Find your HOT SPOT and say your own declaration of how, with God's Grace, you will overcome your "unexpected grief."

Grace Nugget

~

"However, Over Time."

Grace Moment

Crying is a way your eyes speak when your mouth can't explain how broken your heart is.

-Unknown

Grace Reflections (Notes)

_____

_____

_____

_____

_____

_____

_____

_____

_____

_____

_____

_____

_____

_____

_____

_____

Grace Reflections (Cont'd)

Grace Reflections (Cont'd)

Grace Reflections (Cont'd)

Chapter Three

Grieving Over the Loss of a Loved One

"Help for the Broken-Hearted."

The death of a loved one can be an indescribable thing, compound with numbness, a feeling of void, just an unthinkable thing ~ until it happens. It's a shaking of your inner peace and can become a "fight or flight" situation, in some cases. It takes purposed will to find the strength and courage to work through this sadness and the belief that you eventually will make it to the other side of acceptance, self-care, and living again. Over the twenty plus years of caring for and assisting families through this thing called "grief," I've learned that we have been made to endure, to overcome, and to begin again. I have found that we will all get a turn on this merry-go-round of grief and this see-saw of emotions.

You see, the seven emotional stages of grief are usually: shock, disbelief, denial, bargaining, guilt, depression, and acceptance. So all of these stages can lead us down an emotional, physical, and social journey in our lives that we have to deal with. We can find ourselves or hear other people say, "I don't know what I would do without my mama or my husband. Oh Lord, I would have to be put away if my child died, right?" I'm here to tell you that the strength God instilled in us to walk through this trauma is AMAZING. When people ask me, "Deborah, how do you do this? Day after day? Year after year? Family after family?" I tell them all the time, "God is just AMAZING!"

There is no easy way to grieve; it's a process that just has to run its course, over and over, and over again. Everyone reacts differently to grief, and over time will find personal coping techniques that will help them travel the ups and downs of this pain. Now, that's not to say this thing called grief is a walk in the park. There can be intensity and a depth of grieving that only prayer and counseling is needed to get you through. As women and being such emotional beings, we grieve with all our emotions on our shoulders, but the men in our lives most of the time, hold their emotions and hide their true feelings. In doing that, they seldom get a chance to grieve properly until there is such a buildup, that it could become unhealthy.

If we look back over our lives, we can write a list of loved ones that have gone before us, and we are still here to talk about it. I've had my share of deaths. My daddy, "Juke" was struck and killed by a vehicle, my close friend was driving, my younger sister, Beverly passed of an aneurysm, my two brothers, David Lee and Ronnie passed of cancer, my dear mother passed on the Friday before Mother's Day, and my baby sister, Jeanette, passed in her sleep, four months after mama died. Lord Mercy, God is just AMAZING, I tell you.

Losing a loved one is something we live with every day after they have departed this earth. There is not a day; I don't think of all my family members that have taken that journey. Whether the death was anticipated, unexpected, or traumatic, they are thought of every day.

I have found over the years that out of death, comes so much life. To make things easier for yourself and family, find ways to honor and remember our loved one. Try cooking their favorite meal, listening to their favorite music, or just sitting down and writing them a letter of how much you love and miss them. These are a few self-help tools that can aid you tremendously on this grief journey.

When we would travel to Connecticut to visit my father-in-love, I would go into his bedroom, where I can find my mother-in-love's bottle of perfume, her hairbrush and comb that is still on the dresser, to this day, seventeen years later. You see, our love Minnie Jean, passed on Valentine's Day. The first few years after her death, was the most difficult for my husband, which made it the most difficult for me. I had to quickly figure out how to care for my husband during this time every year, and we decided to pull away to have a Day of Love in honor of our love, Minnie Jean. Remember, there is so much more life to live after the loss of your loved one. And it's a journey that you will never have to walk alone.

When dealing with a family that has experienced death by

murder or trauma, such as an accident or suicide, there are just no words to explain or comfort for the most part, it's just unexplainable. And it is during these deaths that I hold on to the scripture: Deuteronomy 29:29, *"The Lord our God has secrets known to no one. We are not accountable for them, but we and our children are accountable forever for all that He has revealed to us, so that we may obey all the terms of these instructions."* New Living Translation Bible

Grief is to each person, like a fingerprint or snowflake, no two people or families will grieve the same way. The pain of losing your loved one or the joy of their memory can be triggered over and over again by a familiar smell or sound, the breeze, someone's look, anything; it can almost feel like a sneak attack.

Let's be determined to accept our grief and continue to live our life to honor our loved one gone before us. Even though death comes, your love will never go away. Love is much stronger than death, and always remember, there is so much more life to live after death.

Grace Nugget

~

"Look upon and cherish your loved ones now,
For if you wait until later, they may be gone."

Grace Moment

When someone you love dies, the love between you never dies. Love is eternal. Love is in the part of us that never dies. The Bible says that to be absent from the body is to be present with the Lord. Your loved one still very much exists. And so does our love. Love is eternal.

-Topaz

Grace Reflections (Notes)

_____

_____

_____

_____

_____

_____

_____

_____

_____

_____

_____

_____

_____

_____

_____

_____

Grace Reflections (Cont'd)

_____

_____

_____

_____

_____

_____

_____

_____

_____

_____

_____

_____

_____

_____

_____

Grace Reflections (Cont'd)

Grace Reflections (Cont'd)

Chapter Four

Grieving Over The Past

"Use Your Past For Positive Purpose."

Grieving over the past is like anything else you have to accept, acknowledge and press through. Past grief can be something that happened in your childhood, your adulthood, or even a day ago; the past is the past, no matter how long it has been. It's like a wound that we pamper, protect, and apply a bandage every time it re-opens. Learning to process our past is an unavoidable step if we want to move forward to become a whole and free individual.

As an adult today, I think of all the woulda, shoulda, coulda, right? Don't you? We all think about those things and ask, "What if I had done it this way or said it that way?" When it's all said and done, we have to grow from our broken past and use all the hurtful pieces, with God's help, as stepping stones of wisdom, clarity, and simply as a way to help others.

How many times have you said or heard someone say to their children, "I've already gone through what you are doing, and it's not worth it." We can all raise both hands to that phrase. Most of the time, the past is like a big giant, hovering over us trying to keep us captive. At some point, you have to say, "Enough is enough," and share your past life and uncomfortable journey with others.

Some years ago at work, I picked up the telephone and on the other end was a young mother, contemplating aborting a second child, but didn't really want to go through with it. At that point, I knew I had to share my story with her about how God saved my son from my womb. You see, I had a traumatic experience at seventeen years old, as a pregnant teenager who was college bound. I had a boyfriend of five years who left all responsibility of fatherhood, and I just could not come to grips with letting my Mama know I was pregnant, so I thought abortion was my only option ~ BUT GOD! After spending time with the young lady over the telephone and sharing my relatable journey, the blessing of having my son with me, and praying for her and with her, she decided to give her unborn child a chance. Months later, she called back to let me know that her little girl was born and she wanted to put her on the list for baby dedication. Lord, thank you for allowing me to use my painful past for your positive purpose, and even more powerful, God allowed my boss to be in his office to witness this blessing. I often let people know that God has cleaned me up so well, you wouldn't believe who I really am if I told you.

The devil meant for me to be a drunk-on drugs, homeless, penniless, no self-esteem, and worthless. However, God's loving Grace has overshadowed you and me, to look the opposite of all these characteristics. There is power in a painful past, and it is a tool to catapult us right into a positive overflowing new beginning ~ whether you are twenty, fifty, or eighty years old. If you are still sane and breathing, it can be done.

I look back on my life today and see God's hedge of protection, even with my past grief. So many times, we ask God to put His hedge of protection around us, and then we question the hedge. And even when we don't have sense enough to ask, it's there. Every time I look in the mirror, I see a miracle because of that hedge. Evidently, what the devil meant for evil, God turned it around for my good and His Glory.

Let's take a moment to decree and declare that our past hurts and unstable issues can't hold us back any longer. Let's share our stories with trustworthy family and friends, journal your past into a better future, get emotional help, and just be determined to stay free from those past shackles.

Grace Nugget

~

"Don't Question the Hedge."

Grace Moment

Do not brood over your past mistakes and failures, as this will only fill your mind with grief, regret, and depression. Do not repeat them in the future.

-Swami Sivananda

Grace Reflections (Notes)

_____

_____

_____

_____

_____

_____

_____

_____

_____

_____

_____

_____

_____

_____

_____

Grace Reflections (Cont'd)

Grace Reflections (Cont'd)

Grace Reflections (Cont'd)

Chapter Five

Grieving Over Self Shame

"Some Things You Did."

This chapter is just a great piggyback on the chapter before. We had to take a look at our past grief, now we have to look at our own self-shames, and we ALL have them. Don't look at me or your neighbor, look right at "The Man in the Mirror," a phrase of deliverance, right from Michael Jackson, himself. He said, "I'm looking at the man in the mirror, I'm asking him to change his ways."

"Lord Mercy," a lot of our self-shame will come directly from things that we have done, and guess what? People know about them. Now, we are grown up and looking like a good Christian, and you hear a voice say, "I know what you did last summer." And guess what again? People are quick to remind you of what you have done, how badly you behaved, and about all the folks you double-crossed. *"You done messed around and stole that money; slept with that girl's husband; abused your child; or lied on Ms. Shirley down the street."* Let's be honest, there are just some guilt and shames that we are praying, Lord, please keep them covered, please don't expose me. Am I right? Me too!!! Mercy Lord!

Guilt and shame are tricky feelings and, in my opinion, somewhat of the same emotion. While it may be possible to feel guilt without shame, we cannot feel shame without guilt. Shame is a robber of our peace, our happiness, and our self-confidence. It can keep us in an up and down relationship, mentally unhealthy, and unsure of ourselves. There have been many days I've thought back over my earlier years and wish I could change a lot of things about how I would treat people who were not very nice to me, those who teased and did ill will towards me. It wasn't pretty, and my mouth was vicious. The scripture, "Lord create in me a clean heart and renew a right spirit within me," that's my scripture. When it seemed the worst, you will have to remember, that God can take the ugliest caterpillar and turn them into the most beautiful butterflies.

My sister Beverly moved away from the entire family and cut herself off from everyone except my brother, Skip. Over the years after her move, it started weighing heavily on my heart, so I started asking God, "Was her move due to all the teasing and unkind words that I would say to her?" I hadn't seen my sister in years, and my heart was broken and so sad because Beverly and I missed out on crossing the bridge to get back to one another. She refused most of my phone calls, cards of repentance, showers of love, and my holiday greeting cards were never acknowledged with a note of thank you or anything. I would often say that I'm going to seek Beverly's forgiveness and hash it out, but year after year passed with no resolve. When I receive the call that my sister was found dead in her apartment due to an aneurysm, I spiraled into self-shame. Shame on me for acting as if I had a lifetime to get things right; Shame on me for caring for everyone else and not my younger sister; SHAME ON ME! This was a tough shame pill to swallow, but through all the pain and shock, God gave me forgiveness, peace, and assurance that Beverly was okay.

When clearing out Beverly's apartment, I asked God to let me have something of hers that would give me a clear look at who she was and how she lived. He led me to a collection of writings that my sister began putting together, as early as 1985 and my favorite poem of hers is entitled, "RAIN!" It was so beautiful that I had it printed on her funeral program. At that point, all I could do was fall to her bed and say, "Thank You, God!" God blessed me even the more; He let me see a few of my opened cards that she had on her dresser and a few cards that our Mother had sent. She lived her life to the fullest and God was all she needed to do that. You see, God blessed my sister to create a wonderful life for herself as a Chef at a local restaurant in Richmond, called The White Dog. She was known for her great preparation of foods and desserts, particularly her "award-winning" Bread Pudding drizzled with Caramel and Hard Whisky Sauce. Now, I don't know about you, but I sure wish I had me some of that! She was so loved by many and respected for her care and loyalty to her friends, which was a great comfort to our hearts as well. I have learned so much from Beverly's death and have vowed to follow my heart, to seek forgiveness and resolution immediately when needed.

In recent years, on December 22nd, Beverly's Heavenly Anniversary, I spend the morning in prayer and thanking God for her life and finding joy in reading over a few of her writings and poems. Listen, Beverly was more in touch with herself, her life, and her well-being than any of us thought. God knew where she was and what she had needed, and that's all that mattered. He is so gracious and loving, and when my sister passed, she was not alone; God was and is with her.

Grace Nugget

~

"You Will Learn More About A Person In Their Death, Then You Knew About Them In Their Life."

Grace Moment

There is no shame in crying
There is no shame of feeling sad
There is no shame in grieving
For the loved ones you once had
There is no shame of hurting
There is no shame of sorrow
Grief has no time limit
Could be today could be tomorrow
There is no shame in silence
There is no shame in tears
It may take a while
Days or months or years
Remember, we all are different
No one grieves the same
But however long it takes,
Remember there is no shame.

-John F. Connor

Grace Reflections (Notes)

Grace Reflections (Cont'd)

_____

_____

_____

_____

_____

_____

_____

_____

_____

_____

_____

_____

_____

_____

_____

Grace Reflections (Cont'd)

Grace Reflections (Cont'd)

Chapter Six

Grieving Over A Broken Relationship

"It Takes Work."

Yes, a broken relationship is a grief! And most specialists in this field will tell you that there are various stages to a broken relationship, which are some of the same emotions mentioned before, such as Anger, Bargaining, Depression, and Denial. Now, this is one subject we can all relate to. Some of us have fewer than others, but we all have had our share. A lost or broken relationship can put you in such a downward spiral, until you look up and say, "I have got to get it together." These emotions can have you asking yourself, "What's wrong with me? What did I do wrong? How can I be a better person? Am I right? We have all asked ourselves these similar questions, as we evaluate this grief.

From our birth, throughout our childhood, as an adult, God made us in His image and LOVE is something we do so naturally. To love is to be vulnerable and easily hurt by people we love the most and who love us the most. It's a relationship breakup that most of the time makes you feel terrible. Now, I know we all may have one or two relationships that we say, "See ya, wouldn't want to be ya," but not nine, ten, eleven relationships. At that point, you may want to start checking on your personality and actions ~ looking at the man in the mirror again.

Have you ever wanted a relationship to work out so badly that you compromised everything about yourself? Everything that you declared you would never do, you did. Making up in your mind that you are never going through this mess anymore, and you do. In life, there are just some relationships that we will have to let go; those that drain us and don't replenish, relationships that are toxic, overpowering, and just sinful ~ they must go! Now, that does not mean that we don't love them to pieces, it just means that some things are just too big for us and it is a job for God, give it over to Him and leave it there.

And then, there are those relationships we have to get enough strength to fight for our marriage, a family member, or a close friend to name a few. I've learned that when I'm really putting in an effort to save a relationship, it has to go into a "cool down" or "timeout" period. Yes, that's right, TIMEOUT, to take a break, time for rest, away from one's usual work (Merriam Webster Dictionary). We have gotten on each other's nerves, and at times, I put myself in time out, because I know, I'm a little touched and can take people to the edge as well. You too!

Listen, for me as a mother, there is nothing more perplexed and disheartening than a broken relationship between a parent and child. A mom and son, a dad and daughter, or vice versa, it can be very painful. It makes you think about, where did I go wrong, what could I have done differently, or am I really the problem? You see, over and over again, in this thing called grief, if we are honest with ourselves, we will be asking and rehearsing a lot of questions and scenarios in our minds and hearts, which is a great checkpoint and balance. As adults, when there are young children around, it's very important not to taint their spirit or grieve their tender heart with grown-up fussing, fighting, or disagreements. This breached relationship can put you and the child in a space of confusion, self-doubt, and awkwardness.

Remember, I mentioned there are some relationships you have to fight for? Well, for me, this is one of them. Fighting for my children is never an option, it's never a question of giving up on them, I will never throw in the towel, even when I feel knock out on the canvas. This is when I have to rely on the song, "Like A Bridge Over Troubled Waters, I Will Lay Me Down." God has to fix this thing; only He can help us sort these things out. And like I tell people all the time, "I don't know when God is going to do it; I don't know how He is going to do it, but He will!

Thy Will Be Done, Oh God, Thy Will Be Done! With prayer, patience, and the power of God, what looked impossible will one day be an overcoming testimony (your true story) to help someone else. Time and a still posture is the key, be still and wait if it's meant to be. There will be many learning and growing opportunities to help us mature and stretch in a big way. These things will give us a small glimpse of what God's Agape Love, Unconditional Love, which God has for us, really looks like.

Grace Nugget

~

"Work at Being the Loving Person,
You Want in Your Life."

Grace Moment

I'd like the memory of me to be a happy one. I'd like to leave an afterglow of smiles when life is done.

-Unknown Author

Grace Reflections (Notes)

Grace Reflections (Cont'd)

Grace Reflections (Cont'd)

_____

_____

_____

_____

_____

_____

_____

_____

_____

_____

_____

_____

_____

_____

Grace Reflections (Cont'd)

Chapter Seven

Grieving Over Hardships

"We Are More Alike Than We Think."

Hardship ~ a situation in which your life is difficult or unpleasant; or a thing hard to bear, specific cause of discomfort or suffering, as poverty or pain. (Dictionary.com)

Now, here is another subject at the top of everyone's list. Yes ~ you, me, our family and our friends. If you really think about it, our hardship situations are things we choose not to share, unless we absolutely have to, as a last result because our backs are up against a wall.

A lot of time, due to pride, embarrassment, or shame, we tend to keep our hardship secrets to ourselves, conditioning our minds to think, we are the only ones going through and enduring this type of "super special" hardship. It's easy to shut yourself in and close out the help that is right in front of you.

Listen, if we are honest with ourselves, we bring quite a bit of hardship into our own lives. *"I know I should not have waited three months to pay that bill or at least communicated my hardship with the creditor. You knew you should not have gone out with the guy who was waving his own red flags; or you knew you should have received help for that abuse so that it wouldn't be passed down to your children."* Hello!

Self-inflicted hardships are the ones we participate in; we see them coming. The Holy Spirit that lives within has warned us, or as most people claim, "I should have followed my gut." We get sign after sign, warning after warning, and we don't change the path of the inevitable end ~ Hardship.

This keeps us focused on the situation with no hope, the thought of no way out and the mindset that you are all alone, which is so far from the truth. Of course, many hardships are specific; seem uncommon, and just as individual as we are. *"No temptation has overtaken you but such as is common to man; and God is faithful who will not allow you to be tempted beyond what you are able, but with the temptation will provide the way of escape also, so that you will be able to endure hardship."* (1 Corinthians 10:13). Just think about it, Jesus left the comforts of Heaven and faced the hardships of humanity for us. He has gone through our same temptations and felt our same hardships and sufferings, to deliver us from death by God's Grace. (John 1:14 New International Version).

God doesn't forget our hardships and has crafted us in such a special and unique way, but yet, we are so similar. In doing a little research, we will all deal with one, if not all of the following hardships ~ Loss, Heartache, Sadness,

Fear, Conflict, and Failure.   Can I get a *"Sho You Right!?"*

I've learned that when going through a hardship, sowing seeds of grace, helping and comforting others, has been a way of escape for me to focus more on serving others, as God is taking care of my crisis and hardship. God moved me to overwhelming tears and thanksgiving on the morning of December 7, 2017. I went into a business at 6:30 this morning, and when I pulled out my credit card to pay, the cashier looked at my full name and had the look of shock on her face. She said, "I will never forget your name because you paid a few months ago to help me stay in shelter at a hotel." Lord Mercy, I cried like a baby ~ you see, I had been dealing with my own hardship with an identical family situation. God is just AMAZING!!! As we take care of others, God will take care of us and ours.

There just has to come a time when we share our hardships, our fears, personal failures, and our sufferings. It's at that moment of sharing when Hope will be activated, Grace can be seen, and Help can be dispatched. We all have someone in our lives who will keep our hardships confidential, keep it in prayer, can speak a word of encouragement, lead you in the right direction of overcoming the hardship, and just think, taking you by the hand and walking you out of that hardship!

Grace Nugget

~

"In spite of what you may see and feel,
NEVER stop sowing Seeds of Grace."

Grace Moment

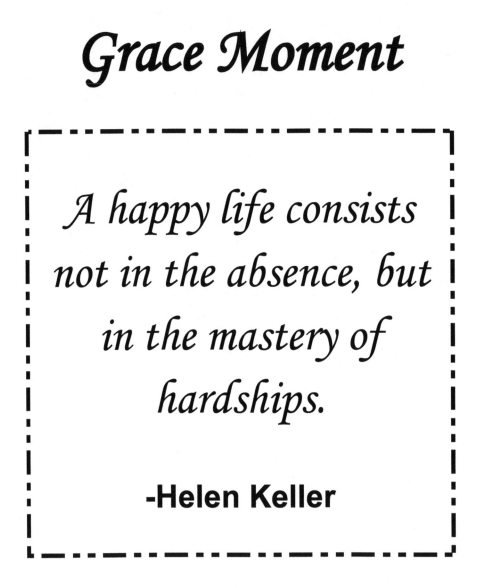

A happy life consists not in the absence, but in the mastery of hardships.

-Helen Keller

Grace Reflections (Notes)

Grace Reflections (Cont'd)

Grace Reflections (Cont'd)

Grace Reflections (Cont'd)

Chapter Eight

Grieving Over Church Hurt

"Know God for Yourself."

Hear ye! Hear ye! Hear ye! Are you listening? Let me whisper something in your ear ~ if you have been in a church for more than a day, a month, for years, and have not experienced church hurt, you are in the wrong church ~ a vibrant congregation, full of God's people. Now, let me just say this right in the beginning of this chapter, I love my Bishop and Pastors, I love ALL of the Seniors, I love my church family and friends. However, from my experience with all of God's jubilance, the soul-stirring, foot tapping, hand clapping, speaking in tongues, and saying all the God Bless ya's, we are all still sinful people, who don't get it right all the time; none of us! See, right there, I've offended some of you already. That's the point!

In the church, some of us are hurt by our own perfect expectation of others, wanting things to run a certain way, or the pastors didn't smile when they walked by you. The church is a hospital, full of sick people, that's why we are there. We come together on a weekly basis to worship and praise God, in a room full of former Thieves, Murderers, Traitors, Abusers, Perjurers, Whoremongers, Fornicators, Drunkards, Idolaters, Liars, Drug Addicts, Drug Dealers ~

Shall I Go On? God speaks about all of us in the B-I-B-L-E, Revelation 21:8; and it's not a pretty ending but THANK GOD for His Grace!

Now, please don't get me wrong. I can still hear one of my Spiritual Mothers singing, "Don't You Want To Be A Part Of The Kingdom, Don't You Want To Be A Part Of The Kingdom, Don't You Want To Be A Part Of The Kingdom, Come On Everybody!" I was a babe in Christ when she would sing that song to me every day, at the Navy Exchange Headquarters. She was lovingly watering the deep seed that had been planted in my spirit that I was fighting tooth and nail, not to let grow.

As a lover of God for more than twenty-three years and as an employee at a church, for approximately twenty years, I've seen and experienced what I call the 3-Ds of dealing with church hurt ~ ***Disagreement, Disappointment, and Division***. It's going to happen; you know why ~ because these are some of the things that happen within a "loving family." There may be a season we just don't get along, we don't want to play together, or we have a hard time communicating. Listen, I'm one of ten children in my family, and we had (and still have) Disagreements, Disappointments, and Division, so how much more do you think it would happen within a church congregation of all sizes?

God is just AMAZING; He has given us a complete manual ~ The Bible, a perfect tool to walk through every grief, every challenge, and the 3-D's (Disagreement, Disappointment, and Division). Like my Spiritual Mother would tell us, "You are not going to be a Big Dummy, sit down and read The Word." LOL, which was some of the best advice I've ever received.

It's our responsibility to stay in God's manual daily seeking His face, asking for a clean heart and a renewed spirit within us. (Psalm 51:10)

To be even more responsible and accountable, be deliberate in pursuing the perseverance it will take to work past what you see and work on being the example you would like to see in others. I often ask God to help me grow in my patience, maturity, forgiveness, grace, and mercy towards others, and in asking for all of that ~ REPENTANCE is a daily task. We have to learn that being like Jesus, we must become the face of GRACE. God knows, we are not perfect and can sometimes be the reason we become hurt and broken.

I'm so grateful for the people in my life that I can glean from those who have lived longer and are much wiser. It's very important to find that kind of accountability balance from friends, who can keep you in check, help you see straight, and let you flat out know when you are wrong. In this "church hurt" journey, you are just going to have to say, "Suu My Lew," a made-up phrase from my spiritual mother, which simply means, "don't worry about it, let it go, move on!" And another suggestion, try knowing Jesus for yourself ~ learn from Him, what to and what not to do; let Jesus be your perfect example, not man. And lastly, you don't have to keep a tally of your wrongs and hurts, El Roi, the one who knows and sees everything, will keep up with that. So, while He's handling our business, we have to rise and use the antidote for Grieving Over Church Hurt ~ which in my opinion, is Prayer, Praise, and Pressing Through ~ knowing that God is in the business of restoring our church's hurt ~ another great gesture of God's Grace.

Grace Nugget

~

"The B-I-B-L-E, that's the Book for me;
I know I am, I'm sure I am, The B-I-B-L-E!"

Grace Moment

We rejoice in our Sufferings, knowing that suffering produces Endurance, and endurance produces Character, and character produces Hope.

-Romans 5:3-4

Grace Reflections (Notes)

Grace Reflections (Cont'd)

Grace Reflections (Cont'd)

_____

_____

_____

_____

_____

_____

_____

_____

_____

_____

_____

_____

_____

_____

Grace Reflections (Cont'd)

Grace Moment

A friend who can be silent with us in a moment of despair or confusion, who can stay with us in an hour of grief and bereavement, who can tolerate not knowing, not curing, not healing and face with us the reality of our powerlessness, that is a friend who cares.

-Henri J. M. Nouwen

Grace Reflections (Notes)

Grace Moment

There is a sacredness in tears. They are not the mark of weakness, but of power. They speak more eloquently than ten thousand tongues. They are messengers of overwhelming grief and unspeakable love.

-Washington Irving

Grace Reflections (Notes)

Grace Moment

Moments when you realize nothing will ever be the same and time is divided into two parts, before this and after this.

-Author Unknown

Grace Reflections (Notes)

Grace Moment

There is purpose in our pain and power in our process ~ God is not done with us yet,
PRESS ON!

-Deborah Juniper-Frye

Grace Reflections (Notes)

Grace Moment

Listen, even when we drop the ball, we can RECOVER, Pick it up and RUN again!

- Deborah Juniper-Frye

Grace Reflections (Notes)

Grace Moment

A grieving heart is full of emotions, struggles, and great despair. Hold on to Love, Hope, and Faith.

- Deborah Juniper-Frye

Grace Reflections (Notes)

Grace Moment

It's really okay for there to be times when you stop putting everyone else first and just do what's best for YOU.

-Tracey Leech

Grace Reflections (Notes)

Grace Moment

Sometimes allowing yourself to cry is the scariest thing you'll ever do, and the bravest. It takes courage to face the facts, stare loss in the face, bare your heart, and let it bleed.

-Barbara Johnson

Grace Reflections (Notes)

Nuggets of Grace

However, Over Time.

Don't Question the Hedge.

Stay Blessed and Forever Encouraged.

The best place to grieve is Under Grace.

Death will bring out the best or the worst of who you are.

Work at Being the Loving Person You Want in Your Life.

Your worth in life will show up at the end of your life.
In spite of what you see and feel, NEVER stop sowing seeds of Grace.

Look up and cherish your loved ones now, for if you wait until later, they may be gone.

Death has a way of making you do things you had no thought of doing in the beginning.

Nuggets of Grace (Cont'd)

Let's stay GRATEFUL with love in our heart and a "Hallelujah Amen Smile" on our face; He will work all things out for our good - He's AMAZING.

Let's GO - NEW Day, New Hope, and New Purpose - Thank You Father for allowing US TO BEGIN AGAIN.

Take advantage of the new GRACE and MERCY, Let Him refresh your mind, body, and soul with His AMAZING LOVE.

You sometimes will learn more about a person in their death, than you knew about them in their life.

No matter what - put a smile on your face and DON'T STOP PRESSING FORWARD.

Thoughts of Conclusion

1. You are not alone on this grief journey.

2. It takes courage to fight through grief and despair intentionally.

3. There is so much Good Grace in grief.

4. We grieve for something in our life every day and don't realize it.

5. Don't miss the moment of Grace.

6. No two people or families grieve the same.

7. Even though your loved one is no longer here, great memories can still be made in their honor.

8. Love, Hope, Faith, Trust ~ a great flashlight to carry when the path becomes a little dark.

Your Thoughts of Conclusion (Notes)

Your Thoughts of Conclusion (Cont'd)

_____

_____

_____

_____

_____

_____

_____

_____

_____

_____

_____

_____

_____

_____

_____

Your Thoughts of Conclusion (Cont'd)

Your Thoughts of Conclusion (Cont'd)

Resource Page

Grief Care Consulting
bit.ly/GriefCareConsulting
@Griefcareconsulting
dfrye.gcc@gmail.com

National Suicide Prevention Lifeline
1-800-273-8255

Parents Stress Hotline
1-800-632-8188

Resources for Survivors of Suicide
www.forsuicidesurvivors.org

TAPS ~ Tragedy Assistance Program for Survivors, Inc.
1-800-959-TAPS (8277)

The Consumer Credit Counseling Services
1-800-388-2227

The Grief Recovery Method
https://www.griefrecoverymethod.com
1-800-334-7606

Unspoken Grief
www.UnspokenGrief.com
info@unspokengrief.com

27278323R00066

Made in the USA
Lexington, KY
04 January 2019